mandalas

mandalas

art by

Jeffrey Spahr-Summers

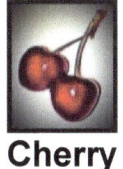

Cherry

Boulder, Colorado

First Edition

Copyright
Jeffrey Spahr-Summers
Cherry Publications 2014, 2019
All Rights Reserved

Books by Jeffrey Spahr-Summers

Poetry

Fear of Heights (1984)
The Cherry Poems (2006)
i believe (2009)
broke before love shack (2009)
jet streaks and power lines (2009)
fifteen minutes (2009)
20 Poems (2014)
6 Days (2014)
History, Poems Written in Chicago 1988-1993 (2014)
no exit (2014)
apple road (2014)

Photography

odaroloc (2009)
green tangerines (2014)
aftereverythingdonebeenflooded.
moon (2014)
mandalas (2014)

Also by Cherry Publications

Non-Practicing Virgin by Marissa Lehto (Poetry, 2014)

Ballad of Todd Last Year by Matt Clifford (Poetry, 2016)

"I had to abandon the idea of the superordinate position of the ego." – Carl Jung

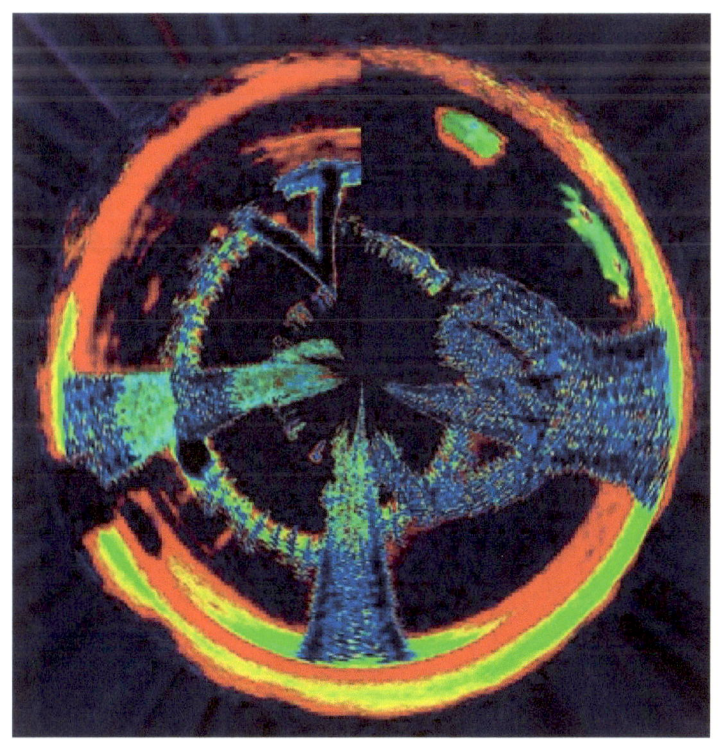

anger

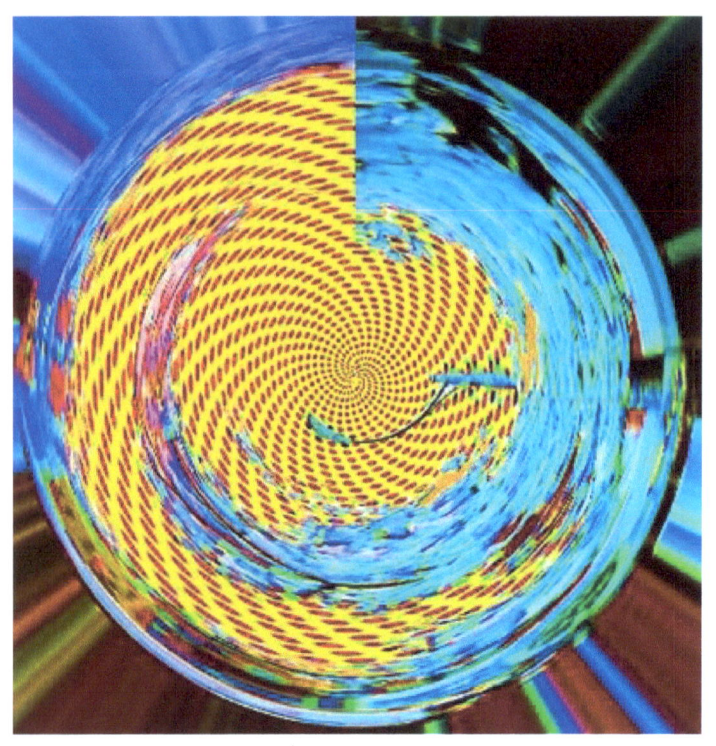

anticipation

anxiety

appearances

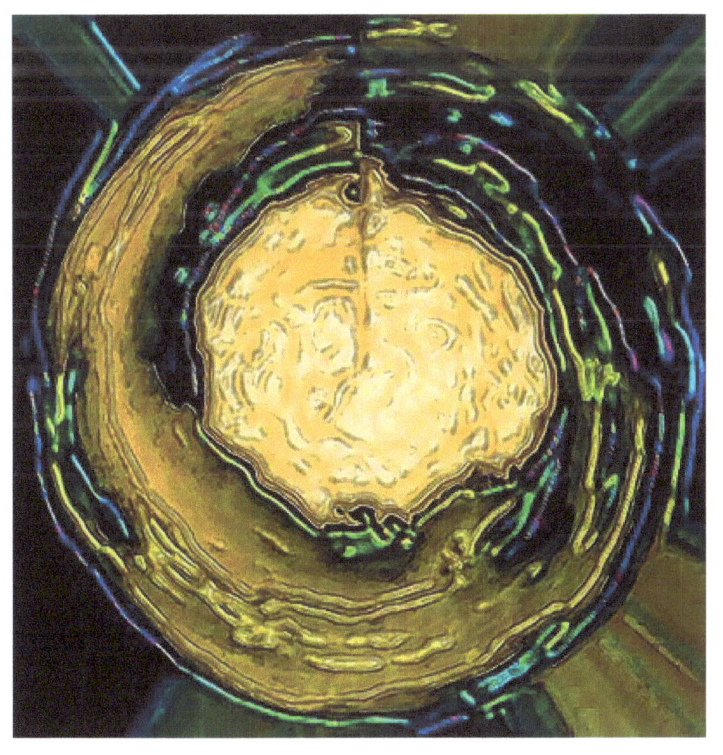

attraction

birth

bliss

change

communication

confusion

creativity

curiosity

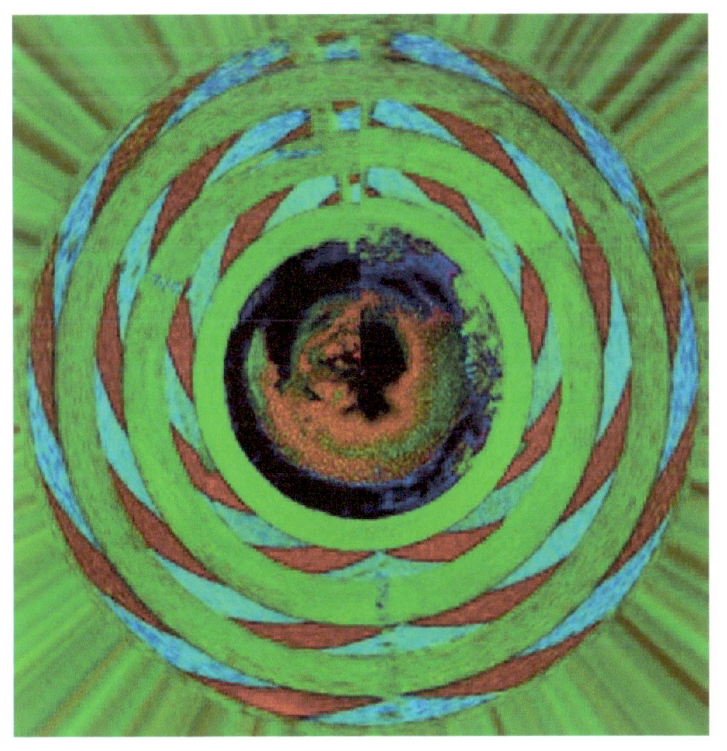

denial

desire

dream

ecstasy

electric

empathy

excitement

fate

fear

flowers in the wind mandala

focus

forgiveness

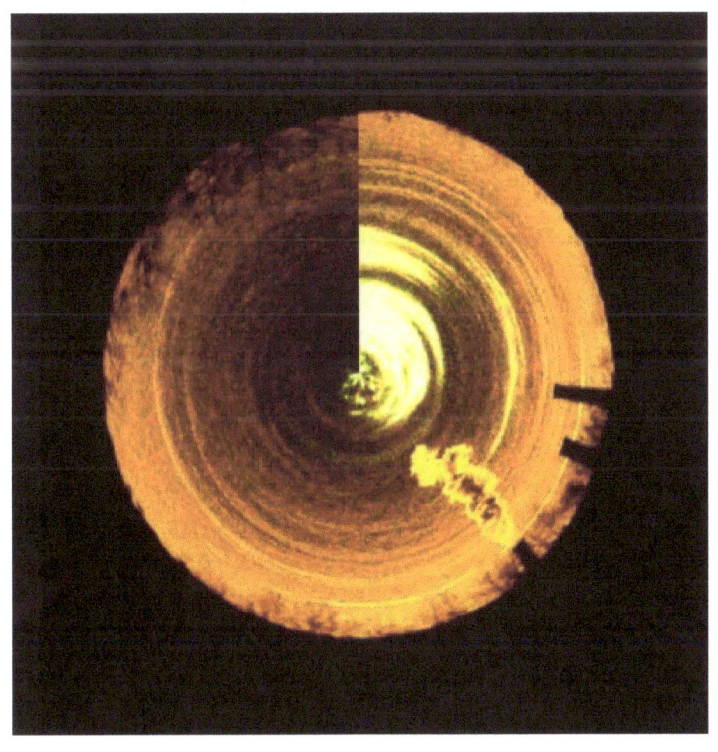

greed

hindsight

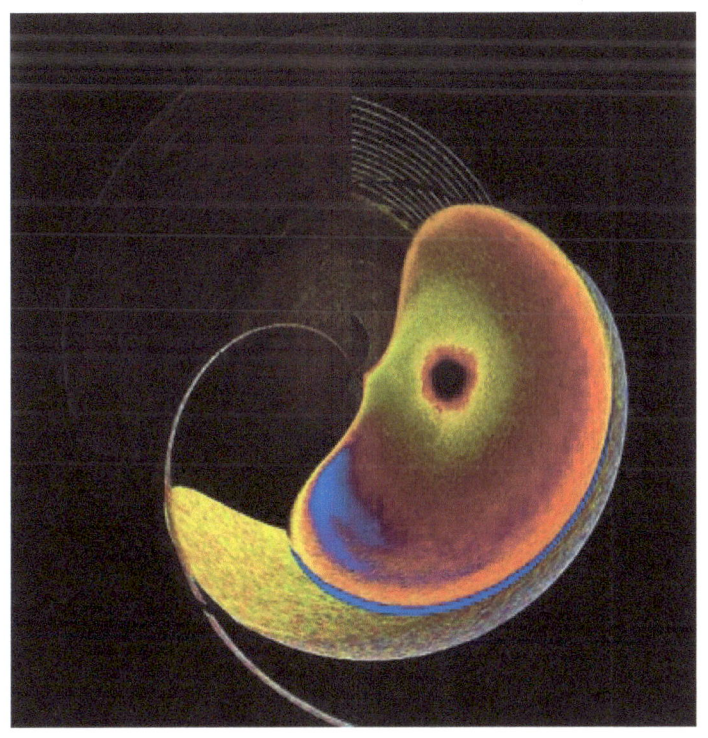

hope

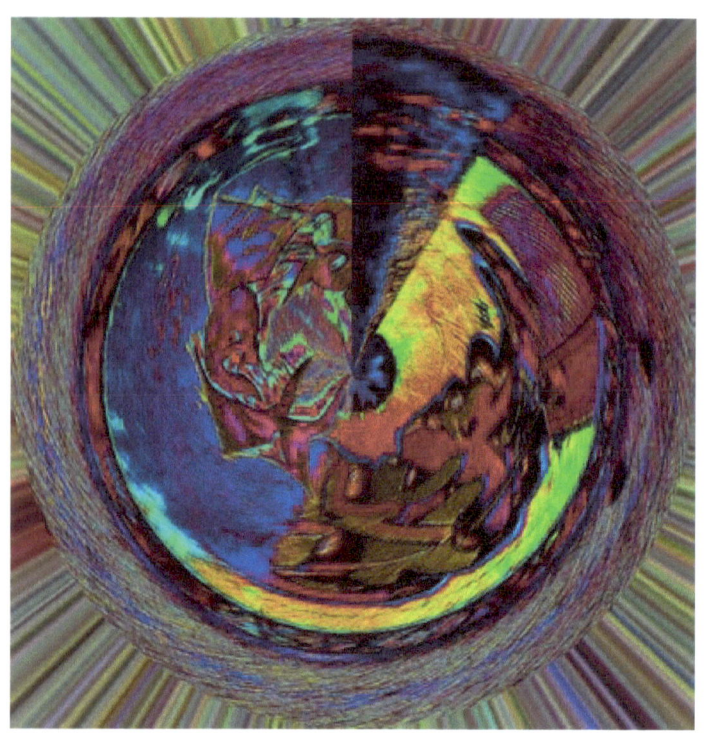

hunger

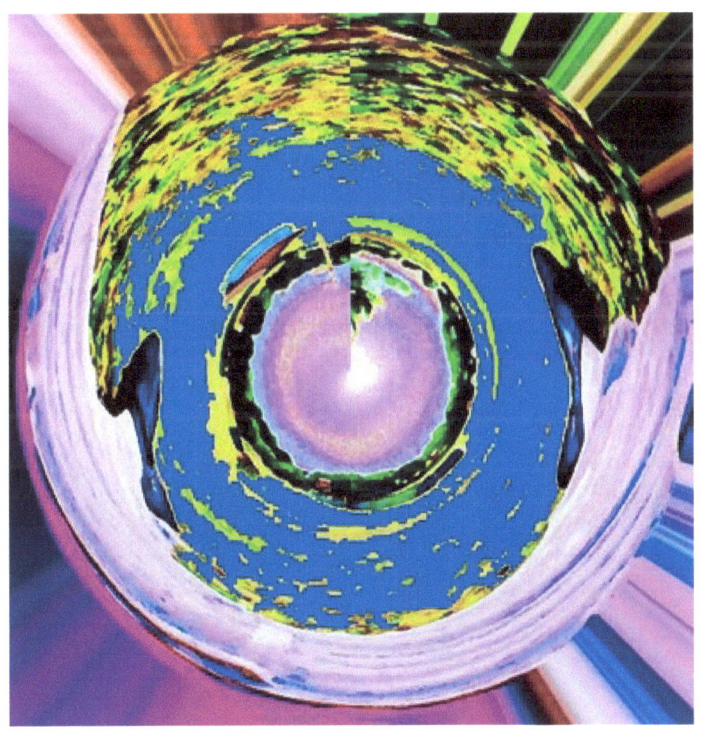

innocence

inspiration

instinct

intuition

irony

jealousy

joy

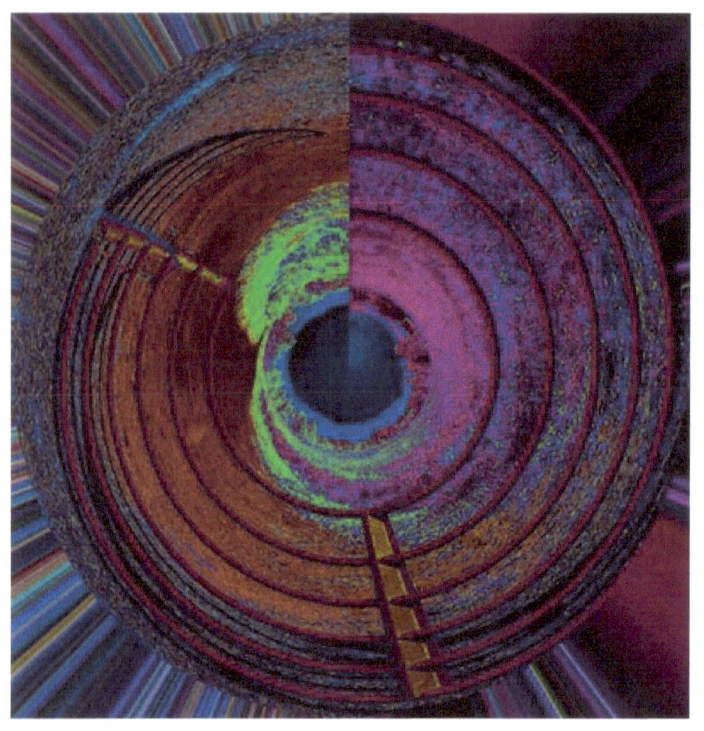

karma

knowledge

loneliness

looking up mandala

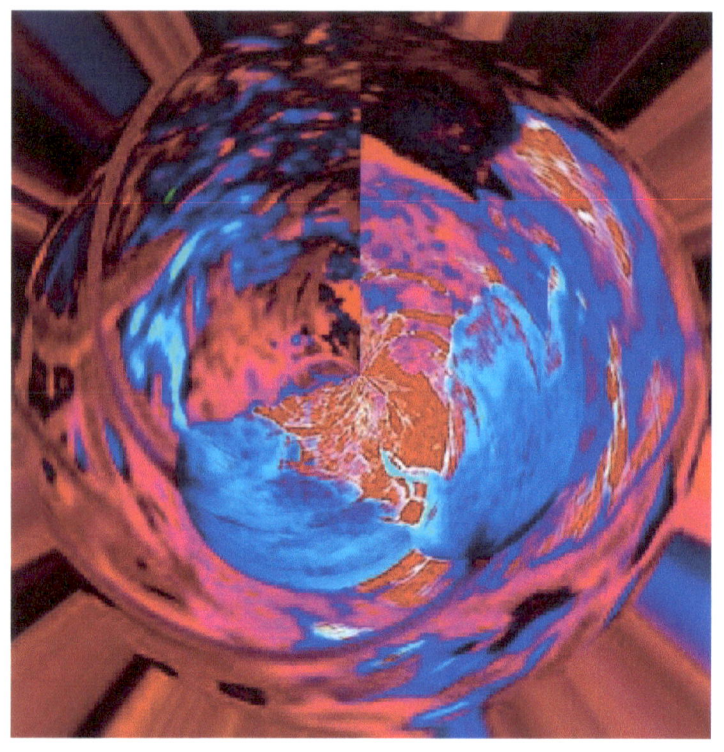

love

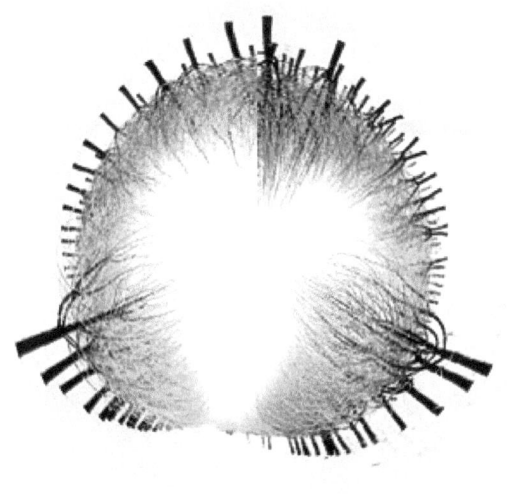

madness

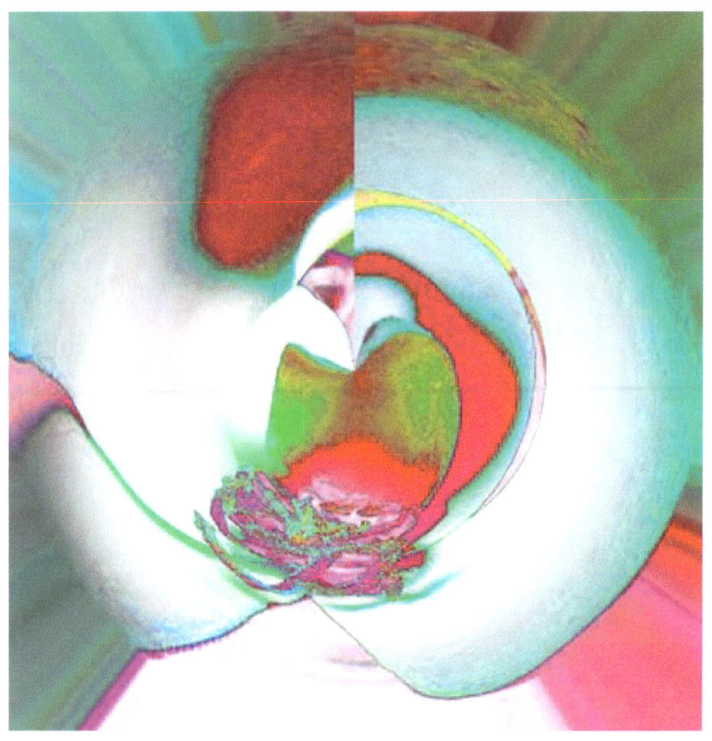

magic

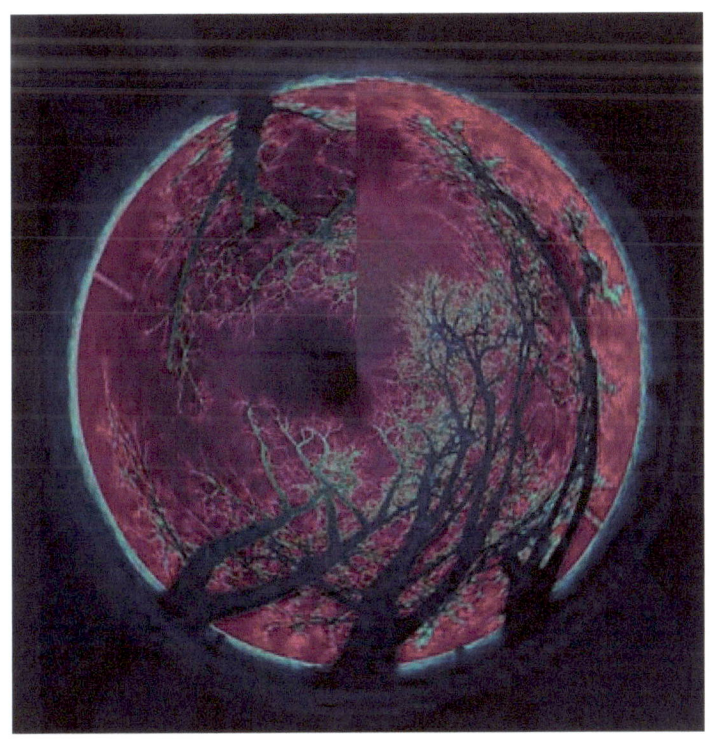

memory

mortality

mystery

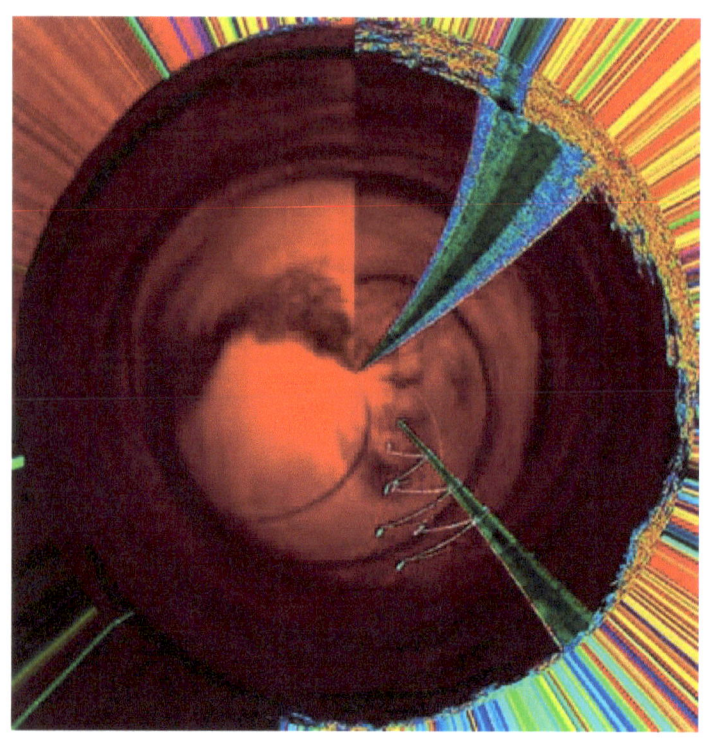

pain

patience

peace

perspective

pride

ramble on mandala

rapture

recognition

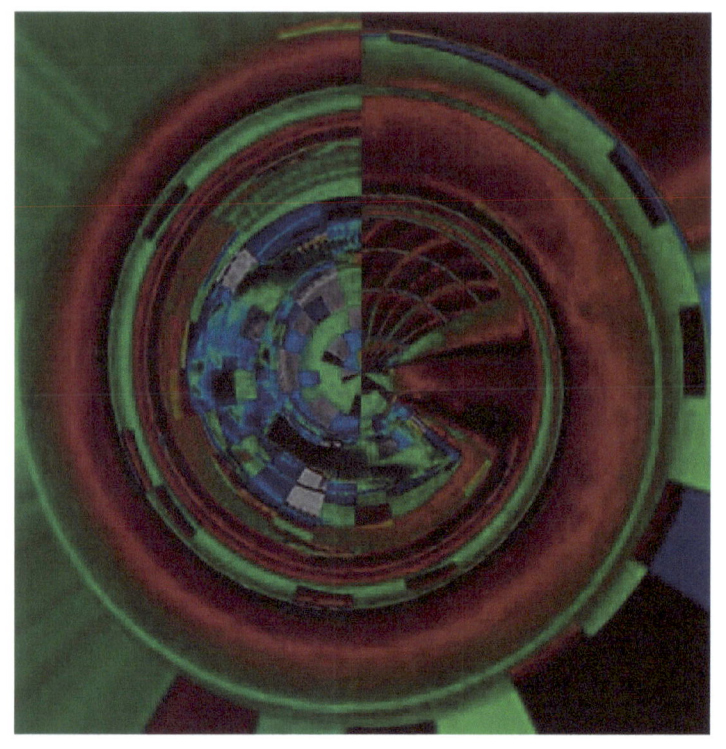

reflection

regret

satisfaction

speed

surprise

terror

the dance is a poem of which
each movement is a world

the essential iron and wine
mandala

the meaning of life mandala

the most important thing in life
is to learn how to give out love
and to let it come in

the most important things in
life arent things mandala

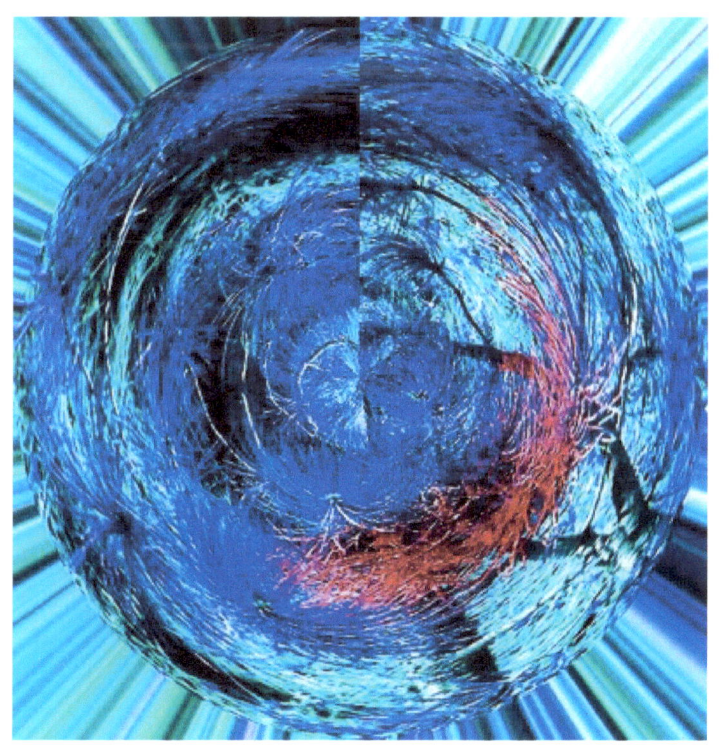

this is the love and friendship mandala

this is the missing you mandala

this is the new beginning mandala

time

www.ingramcontent.com/pod-product-compliance
Lightning Source LLC
Chambersburg PA
CBHW041103180526
45172CB00001B/80